W9-CKI-456

Ocean Life

Kelp

By Lloyd G. Douglas

Welcome Books™

Children's Press®
A Division of Scholastic Inc.
New York / Toronto / London / Auckland / Sydney
Mexico City / New Delhi / Hong Kong
Danbury, Connecticut

Photo Credits: Cover, p. 7 (bottom right) © Ralph A. Clevenger/Corbis; p. 5 © Paul Edmondson/Corbis; p. 7 (top right) © Jeffrey L. Rotman/Corbis; p. 7 (bottom left) © Peter Johnson/Corbis; pp. 7 (top left), 13 © Brandon D. Cole/Corbis; p. 9 © Norbert Wu/Minden Pictures; p. 11 © Bill Curtsinger/Getty Images; p. 15 © Andrew Sallmon/Lonely Planet Images; p. 17 © Hal Beral/Corbis; p. 19 © Michael S. Yamashita/Corbis; p. 21 (Ice Cream Cone) © Comstock Images

Contributing Editor: Shira Laskin
Book Design: Elana Davidian

Library of Congress Cataloging-in-Publication Data

Douglas, Lloyd G.
    Kelp / by Lloyd G. Douglas.
    p. cm. — (Ocean life)
    Includes index.
    ISBN 0-516-25029-9 (lib. bdg.) — ISBN 0-516-23742-X (pbk.)
    1. Kelps—Juvenile literature. 2. Kelp bed ecology—Juvenile literature. I. Title.

    QK569.P5D68 2005
    579.8'87—dc22

                                                    2004010214

Contents

Kelp is a plant.

It grows **underwater**.

There are many different kinds of kelp.

Giant kelp can grow to be more than 200 feet long.

It is the largest plant in the ocean.

9

Kelp can have green or brown leaves.

Kelp plants often grow near each other.

This is called a **kelp forest**.

13

Fish and other animals live in kelp forests.

Some of them use kelp for food.

Some birds eat kelp too.

People **harvest** kelp from the ocean.

Sometimes kelp is used to make ice cream.

It can also be used in paper and toothpaste.

People use kelp for many things.

21

New Words

harvest (**har**-vihst) to pick or gather
kelp (**kelp**) a type of seaweed that can be eaten
    and used to make many things
kelp forest (**kelp for**-ist) an area where many kelp
    plants grow together
underwater (**uhn**-dur-waw-tur) below the surface
    of water

To Find Out More

Books
Life of the Kelp Forest
by Lynn M. Stone
Rourke Publishing

The Hidden Forest
by Jeannie Baker
HarperCollins Children's Book Group

Web Site
Dive Into Worlds Within the Sea
http://ology.amnh.org/marinebiology/divein/index.html
Learn more about kelp and other ocean life and play games
on this Web site.

Index

About the Author
Lloyd G. Douglas writes children's books from his home near the Atlantic Ocean.

Content Consultant
Maria Casas, Marine Research Associate, Graduate School of Oceanography, University of Rhode Island

Reading Consultants
Kris Flynn, Coordinator, Small School District Literacy, The San Diego County Office of Education

Shelly Forys, Certified Reading Recovery Specialist, W.J. Zahnow Elementary School, Waterloo, IL

Paulette Mansell, Certified Reading Recovery Specialist, and Early Literacy Consultant, TX